FROM THE HEART OF AN OLD POET

POETRY

WHEN MY HEART SINGS IT WANTS TO SING OUT LOUD

BY

GARY ADES BOWKER

Dedicated to Gwen

Contents

Acknowledgements

I am indebted to my son G. Griffin Bowker for the hours spent compiling this book of poetry. His technical skills were indispensable in producing the working manuscript and finished product.

Further thanks to my daughter Elizabeth for her support and encouragement in the writing of poetry, and to Carolyn whose love is the foundation of this family.

This edition, dedicated to our daughter Gwen, is a response to a grand person who has inspired the writing of poetry.

Thanks to all those who have contacted me with support in my earlier publications.

.GB.

STRUMMINGS

Notes

Come...Sleep My Love

Today, my love looked so very tired. You know the look,
conversation slows, the head seems too heavy to hold upright,
the eyes look smokey.

The poem is a poem of sympathy. Sleep my love...sleep.

.GB.

Come...Sleep, My Love

Today my love, your eyes looked tired,

where laughter played and light inspired.

I saw sleep that yearned to be,

wrapped in warmth and holding thee.

To light that fire from within,

may sleep be yours, and soon begin.

Quietly now the sands fall fine,

and whispers sleep, "Be thou mine".

.GB.

Notes

Route 2

Route 2 is a highway that begins in Maine, does a fancy dance around the Great Lakes, and ends in the State of Washington.

It is an old automobile trail that transported folk across the upper tier of the U.S.A. from the earliest years of the automobile.

At one time it was designated the *Theodore Roosevelt Highway.*

It was on this highway, in the town of Waterville, Washington, on a snowy night in late December that I walked beside a breathtakingly beautiful girl.

I married her one year later...almost to the day. It was the best decision I have ever made.

I suspect there are books full of stories that point to a certain place with a special person that many point to as the place and time they recognized that this person was...The One!

I did, and to her I dedicate this poem...It's still true.

.GB.

Route 2

There you stood
 in skinny clothes,
bone thin I suppose,
 I saw you there
 ...I remember.

 It was on a day in late December.
The year no longer matters.
Time began as time begins,
where memory often gathers,
 and I...there with you.

Magic minced the air,
Snow bejeweled your raven hair,
might have been anywhere,
but there,
my heart spoke true.

No robin roused to sing,
nor leaf lay lush upon the spring.
I took your hand, you let it stay,
there on that winter day
...on Old Route 2.

.GB.

Notes

The Ring

The Ring is a poem that acknowledges a trait of my life and of my relationships. I think the sense of myself in this poem is found in most people as one digs into the inner self. I've discovered that my position on life has changed over the years. People have come into my life and have moved on, but there are people, and issues that come back to me. I can't explain why, but something in me wants to return. I call it ordained, set aside, deeply important, and though my path has led me away, the path leads back. Life, my life, is an odyssey. There have been storms, gentle days, friends, associates, issues, settings, changes of heart and perspective. But, in all of the changes there are some that emerge...again.

.GB.

The Ring

Strange the path I walk each day,

a path that winds further away.

But, then, circles round and comes back,

Back to its starting ground.

The going out I understand.

Yet, for all the years and many miles,

the path leads here,

and here I am.

Who shapes this path,

who brings it round?

Odd this ordained odyssey,

odyssey ordained in me.

.GB.

Notes

Wishes

The poem *Wishes* pokes a bit of fun at ourselves as we pitch pennies in fountains and ponds while making a wish. We like to light a candle in remembrance of a person in our thoughts. But, I'm not sure either act makes a difference...unless so doing moves us to make some helpful act. A note, a card, a call, a donation in the name of the person or object of our thought is a wonderful outcome of penny or pyre.

There are many acts of kindness and generosity that can be carried out. I will endeavor to carry out the wish or thought the next time I am at the pond or in the narthex where candles give light to a memory still alive.

.GB.

Wishes

To pitch a penny in a pond

and cast a dream most true,

what does such a thing make the heavens do?

 Or, waxen pyres with little fires

and wishes quick to make.

What do such things do...what for heaven's sake?

 There are things we'll never know,

things we misconstrue.

Yet, a silent word is fully heard

....in actions that we take.

.GB.

Notes

Penny Rich

Pennies are the lowest unit of currency in the United States of America. It takes ten pennies to make a dime, and one hundred pennies to make a dollar.

It takes a lot of pennies to have a substantial sum of money.

The poem emphasizes the number of times I think of "you". So many times that I'm instantly rich!

Just a bit of whimsy to describe what "you" mean to "me".

.GB.

Penny Rich

If I got a penny for thinking of you

There'd be hills of pennies that to mountains grew.

The glitter of copper shines like gold

It staggers my mind...the bills I fold.

When I see pennies, I know it's true...

I'm instantly rich...at the thought of you.

.GB.

Notes

Emily's Heart

There hangs on my wall a picture of a heart held securely in a hand. It is painted crimson red on a canvass, bone white and framed in a frame of shaded gold.

It was a gift from a much appreciated friend who sent it to me at a time when my life was in the balance.

As I look at the painting I like to think that the hand is the hand of God, and the heart is mine, for surely it is, perhaps for us all.

Emily speaks with paint on canvass a message greater than words on paper, and I shall be forever grateful.

Thank you, Emily, God bless you.

.GB.

Emily's Heart

Today gained a gift...primrose brushed and penned.
A heart first found deep, within my gifted friend.
It beats upon the page, a plate as white as bone,
Framed with sculpted wood, in fashioned shades of gold.
This heart is, and shall ever be
A living hope...*le grande coeur d' vie.*
Mending now my wounded heart, as in portrait told
Gently held in God's hand, healing in the fold.
The heart shares its living beat, the essence of our soul,
To sound aloud the bells of life, that
    ...on the Sabbath toll.

.GB.

Notes

Ships

Ships is a metaphor for people seeking to track a relationship. All relationships are in constant flux, and are moving toward or away. The relationship might be docked, or kept at a distance.

The task of defining a relationship is a constant process and can never be assumed. In our modern world, ships are tracked from satellites and are advised to steer around storms.

Some relationships have serious issues that bear close attention...much like ships heading toward a storm. Or, perhaps a person standing on a pier seeking a ship carrying a special person.

.GB.

Ships

There bore a speck upon the sea,

sailing to or fro from me?

Can one tell so far away

through morning haze cool and gray?

Eyes see ships that sail afloat,

this eye seeks a single boat.

Ships are symbols of the sea,

signs of souls sailing free.

Whether specks sail into view

waits for time, as most things do.

.GB.

Notes

To Pick a Day

To Pick a Day is an ode to a special woman whose birthday is in
May. The poem was written to be presented on her birthday.
She has been my rock and my love through the years. She is my
blessing. The words here are not hyperbole. Each word and
thought has been fulfilled many times over.

The world of poetry is filled with poems of love and admiration.
Prose can be endearing, but poetry runs deeper. Think of
Elizabeth Barrett Browning's *How Do I Love Thee?* With prose she
could have said very honestly and with much feeling...*I love you.*
But, expressing her love poetically has given Robert Browning and
the world a poem that speaks to the heart of every love in the
world...a love that endures even after death.

And, what of the poem penned by William Butler Yeats, *When You
Are Old.* One cannot read it without feeling the love deep in one's
heart...*How many loved your moments of glad grace, and loved
your beauty with love false or true; but one man loved the pilgrim
soul in you.*

A final word: Shakespeare's Sonnet XVIII set a standard that has
been seldom matched. *Shall I compare thee to a Summer's day?...
Rough winds shake the darling buds of May. But thy eternal
Summer shall not fade...So long lives this, and this gives life to me.*

.GB.

To Pick a Day

If I could pick a day,

it would be the whole of May.

Every day to be with you,

to sing of birth and babies too.

Celebrations of a single day,

beg the space to stay and play

and further bind the time to say

...I adore you.

The flag of life is fast unfurled,

wending years that simply whirled

all around the global cone,

once or twice to dwell alone. But, May means

you in a special way,

that spectacular you, who makes my day,

who has been, and are, my greatest prize.

Poets muse on the finer things

like the beauty your love brings.

You are the flowers that give life worth,

you are the rainbow's arch o'er earth.

And, to have you on this special day

is more that in one day, try as I may to say,

...you are my world.

.GB.

Notes

...Along the Way

...Along the Way shares thoughts of a day when we are no longer with someone who meant so very much to us. It might be a separation of time or it might be a separation of death that offers only the remembrance of that person. We move from place to place to place leaving people who have planted a sweet memory. We have lived with people who are forever gone and are seen only in our memories. The moments of seeing them come in unexpected ways, but they are real and they are felt deep within. We feel the pang of loss, but are flooded with the gratitude for having had them in our lives.

Time takes away, but memories are forever. The good memories we keep. We keep them because they nurture us and carry us through times of hardship and heighten us in times of joy and celebration.

Thank you, I shall always remember you. I will see you along the way.

.GB.

...Along the Way

If there be a day,

where, there along the way

you hear a whisper.

Turn and look to see

If, for a moment it was me.

.GB.

Notes

If Ever a Day

Neil Diamond sang the lyrics to a song called *If You Go Away*. In that song there is a line that states...*but if you stay I'll make you a day like no day has been*. The poem, *Seaside*, was written with the same whimsy. It was written just for fun.

What fun we have at the beach. Time seems to fly, especially when we are in the company of someone very special. It is a day of play that seems to end too soon.

In the song the writer guards against either of the two, going away, and promises that if they stay it will be a day like no day has been...and then promises to make the night as good as the day. In the poem the same sense of the day, and night is expressed.

There are times in life when the sun shines and the moon is at play. A time when everything seems to float on warm air, a time when birds sing and hearts are high.

Such is expressed in this poem.

.GB.

If Ever a Day

With you my friend I would spend
Time upon the shore.
        To play,
And, see on high seagulls fly
Near the ocean door.
        Today,
With sculpting hands our castle stands
Near the briny roar.
        We'll stay,
Just for fun through foam we'll run
And, dance the tidal band.
        All day,
As light fades 'way we'll script a plan
And, scrawl our stay on shifting sand.
        And night,
The night, the night; Is that the sun,
Rising east once more?
        Pure Diamond.

        .GB.

Notes

The Step

Life can change with a single step. A friend once said, "If you take the first step you are already halfway there."

This poem was written for the person that would profit from taking a step toward a new life...with new people. There was nothing written in a book or displayed on a chart that could be better than the simple resolve to take a step in a new direction. And, in so doing claim a life that would offer unlimited opportunity.

We are all confronted with choices. Some will injure us at the deepest level of our lives. And others will lift our spirits and give light to our path.

.GB.

The Step

There is a single step
that changes all our days,
a choice deeply made
to open future ways.
The direction made
on no map or chart,
is the will...to forge a start.
Small it seems,
but with a different goal,
A single step, one single step
...to claim again our soul.

.GB.

Notes

Butterflies

Who has not looked at butterflies and experienced a sense of delight and a tinge of awe. This beautiful creature represents the good of life. They come in myriad varieties and live in most areas of the world.

Butterflies begin as a wormlike creature and go on to shed their pupal skin, metamorphize from a cocoon to become a beautiful creature that flies with protein wings.

The butterfly has flown for fifty million years. Some of today's butterflies migrate across thousands of miles.

Whenever I see a butterfly I am uplifted.

Painters, poets, writers and composers have been moved by, and have written in honor of the butterfly.

Vincent van Gogh stated that his butterfly paintings were symbols of hope.

Butterflies are creatures of transformation...so too are we.

.GB.

Butterflies

Theology,
we might not understand,
but,
we sense something of God
as a butterfly,
flutters to our hand.

.GB.

Notes

Bona Fide

Bona Fide acknowledges the truth of its central point...the occasion of sharing the deepest issues of life with another person do not often come to us. But, when that moment comes it is remembered, cherished and held somewhere deep within.

To be inwardly touched or to deeply touch another, is more valued than mere things acquired for worldly comfort.

Jesus reduces all of the law, all of the ritual, all of theology to this...*love God and love your neighbor as yourself.*

.GB.

Bona Fide

From life comes no greater thing
nor more to one does welcome bring,
than touching true the human soul
as our day's most treasured goal.

We have so many things
that can to us much comfort bring,
but, they will never-never bring
things that make the spirit sing.

To see a heart filled with good,
do all the good we ever could,
to serve down deep a bond of love,
both in this world and from above,
is the cradle of real life
...the credo of Christ's call.

Thus, to meet souls in this place,
to know of love and all God's grace
is the best that this life gives...
for there within, the blest soul lives.

.GB.

Notes

Samaritan

This poem was written for my son upon the attainment of his majority. It was written in the hope that he would treat drinking with respect, and maintain an awareness of its potential consequences.

The poem describes the role of the person who seeing the results of someone who has had too much.

The Good Samaritan is presented as a model for human conduct in a parable found in *Luke 10* of the New Testament. Luke was a medical doctor and concerned with human well-being, perhaps more than any of the other disciples. This parable is perhaps the most cherished parable in the New Testament.

The parable features a person not expected to be of help to the man in need. Others had passed by, others who might well have been expected to be of help.

It is the act of kindness given by someone not required to act that sets this parable apart. It is the heart of the Gospel of Jesus. It is a rule to live by.

We are called to be Samaritans.

.GB.

Samaritan

I'm resting here upon the floor,

I think I'll have just one more.

Then, I'll find my car and drive on home,

it's not far if I don't roam.

My eyes are red and my hands are sore,

If I can just make it to the door.

The crowd is loud, and very rude,

they took my keys and called me "Dude".

"Come back tomorrow and get your keys,

but not tonight, you're on your knees.

We have for you a taxi cab,

who'll take you home,

...we've paid the tab".

.GB.

Notes

Remembering

Every now and then thoughts enter our minds that allow us to see things we have never seen, nor have we ever thought about it. It is a mysterious gift of the mind. It is the seat of creativity. These thoughts are not innovations, they are a completely new thing.

The human mind is complex, far deeper than anything now known.

.GB.

Remembering

Things I've never known
feelings I've never had
from a place I've never been
in the stillness of a silent storm.
Seeing things locked deep
where deeper thoughts I long to keep
of all that never was
in a life never lived
...like a shadow in the night,
this light.

.GB.

Notes

Twelve and Ten

Twelve and Ten is dedicated to all the kids who were friends, and looking back recognize the admiration and respect they shared. I had friends and close cousins who fit such esteem.
As we grew up we were separated by distance, jobs, pilgrimages and vocations...obstacles to seeing and being with one another. But, despite the distance and infrequent meeting I held these lifelong buddies in the highest regard, and look back on the days of twelve and ten with great affection.

.GB.

Twelve and Ten

If I were twelve
and you were ten,

you'd sure be
my best friend,

'cause you're smart
and think things through,

an' there ain't nothin'
you can't do.

You can beat me
in a race,

and climb a tree
at lightnin' pace

But, more than that
it's 'cause you're you,

an' I like you
...I sure do.

When we grow up
I hope we meet,

where grownups gather
and old friends greet.

.GB.

Notes

'Til Never

'Til Never addresses the issue of a poetic understanding of an extremely complex topic. Light is a mystery defined in many ways, not fully understood by science or genius minds.

We explain creation in science with the big bang theory. Religion and myth simply assert that God did it. Simple...God did it. That gives an answer to a question yet to find an answer. Just how did this all come to be? And, where did it come from?

At the very beginning of the Holy Bible among Christians and Jews we find that God created light. Anyone can point out that we have light, and it came from something, somewhere. The answer from our ancestors is that God created it.

Our human minds are not especially content with that answer. We have discovered much about light. Wave and particle theories abound. The color spectrum is astonishing, so are the varieties of light. Some light passes through everything. Some can only be seen with sophisticated technologies.

As a simple poet who understands little of the subtle aspects of issues like the ones raised by science...and not satisfied by a solution that simply says that God did it, this poet marvels at the "what is" rather than the "who did it". And, light is one of the many miracles that dazzle. Velocity varies time. Is space endless? Poets enjoy the freedom to expound.

So, the poem. Time, space, light...all mysteries.

.GB.

'Til Never

It's ten minutes 'til never
will never ever come due?
Will the world remain
when everything's through?
But darkness won't come,
'cause dark is untrue.

Shades of light live in the soul,
living in life to all things extoll.

Shades of light in all cosmic things,
within each atom billions of strings.
Each with a light and, in light it sings.

Ten minutes 'til never
...shear twinklings.

.GB.

Notes

I Corinthians 13: 1-7 & 13 KJV

Of everything written by Saint Paul this passage is his greatest. It is the key to all life, and underlies the basic concept of the Christian life. He distills this passage to three great qualities...faith, hope and love. Reading this chapter makes evident that love is Paul's supreme quality because it is active. It requires active commitment to agape love. It is a love that extends to all things and to all people. It is the active state of love that formed all that is.

The Apostle John wrote in a book of the Holy Bible bearing his name, Chapter 4, verse sixteen that God is love, and in verse nineteen that we love because God first loved us.

It is my observation that people who apply love to the circumstances of life live happier lives.

.GB.

I Corinthians 13: 1-7 & 13

Though I speak with the tongues of men and of angels

and have not love, I am become as sounding brass,

or a tinkling cymbal.

And though I have the gift of prophecy,

and understand all mysteries, and all knowledge;

And though I have all faith, so that I could remove mountains,

and have not love I am nothing.

And, though I sell all my goods to feed the poor,

and though I give my body to be burned and have not love,

it profiteth me nothing. Love suffereth long, and is kind;

Love envieth not; love vaunteth not itself, is not puffed up.

Doth not behave unseemly, seeketh not her own way,

is not easily provoked, thinketh no evil;

Rejoiceth not in iniquity, but rejoiceth in truth;

Beareth all thing, believeth all things hopeth all things,

endureth all things.

And now abideth faith, hope and love, these three;

But the greatest of these is love.

Saint Paul

Notes

Magic

Magic is everywhere. When I think of magical moments I realize that magic appears without expectation or explanation. Magical moments shoot the gamut, from subtle to electrifying. Some magic appears in the moment and some appears as one looks back and realizes that magic happened...and they were there to see it, to feel it and, experience it.

Magic happens to everybody; it happens in every facet of life.

Mazarine is a shade of blue, it describes the light of night where magic often appears.

.GB.

Magic

Magic is a wonderful thing,
crossing the earth like the sweep of a wing.
Where it flies one never knows
as lightning strikes down to the toes.
That's when magic comes 'round.
Shooting the moon, shaking the ground.
Charging the air...where
a look has changed...like wind-blown hair,
unaware, a slight of hand
fooling us where we don't understand.
Sunset and dawn, light paints the sky,
magic performed...we didn't try.
Even at night in deep mazarine,
it comes...quite unseen.
As it arrives it's felt in our bones.
Sometimes in sighs and softspoken tones.

.GB.

Notes

When Next

As you meet me my love, greet me with a kiss. As I come home from a busy day, perhaps a hard day, there is nothing more welcome than your arms around my neck. Your beautiful face close to mine, waiting for a kiss...a kiss that sparks this love, a kiss that stops time and erases the aches. I will hold you for an extra moment, thanking God that it is you I hold.

Never have I been surer of anything.

There is an urgency to love, a deep yearning of the heart. Bobbie Burns in his poem *Red, Red Rose,* said it thus, *As fair thou art, my bonnie lass...and fare thee well...my love is like a melody...I will come again, though it were ten thousand mile.*

.GB.

When Next

When next you see me,

    would your arms seek my neck,

that I might hold thee,

    my heart a captured wreck.

Softly close your misty eyes,

    beneath the warm and waiting skies

...and I shall gently kiss thee.

    .GB.

Notes

This Gentle Dream

One might see something of John Ronald Ruel Tolkien woven into the tapestry of this poem. At the beginning, it was not written with Tolkien in mind, but as the poem developed the thought of Luthien-Tinuviel became the choice in describing the essence of love in this poem.

Tinuviel was the first name Tolkien used to describe Beren's encounter with her. Tinuviel is the nightingale, the sunset maiden singing in the twilight...with whom Beren, a mortal, fell in love. Later Tokien used the name Luthien, which means blossom, enchantress, the fairest maiden in all of the land. The name might have been derived from the Old English name Lufien which is a synonym for love.

The shady grove of the poem is a place where Tinuviel might be found, and she might be singing her love to sleep.

The tale of Luthien and Beren is a long and adventurous tale which ends in death for them both, but being myth there was a way for Luthien to restore Beren to life. Luthien was given a choice in which she chose to live with Beren as a mortal, and thus face eventual death.

It is a tale that has endured in mythology. Luthien and Beren gave the world a story of love as real as Romeo and Juliet.

When love is authentic, it is forever. Love is not perfect as lived by mortals, but it is the one thing that endures... above all else.

.GB.

This Gentle Dream

Kiss me to sleep my love
and soothe my yearning heart.
I long to feel your touch
a song in every part.
As sings the nightingale,
and here makes a nest.
Come to me my Luthien,
of all you are the best.
Kiss me to sleep my love
in some shady grove,
my head upon your lap,
and I in sweet repose.

.GB.

Notes

Buzzing Bee, Fox and Tree

Quiet walks are not really quiet. There is much that emerges during a quiet walk. As the demands of life are stilled thoughts are quietly heard. Inner voices speak that are good for the heart, mind and soul.

It is possible that more important decisions are made in the course of a walk than in any other way. Walking frees the mind, lifts the spirit and quiets the soul.

There is an old poem by Amary Hare titled *Walking at Night, "My face is wet with rain...but my heart singing...alone on the road I love of yore...to walk in the wet a while...and see the slow delight."*

.GB.

Buzzing Bee, Fox and Tree

It came by some friendly way,

whispers of light that seemed to say,

a word, but not betray...who,

maybe you, in the buzz

of bees and things nature does.

I like those quiet walks,

where words wish well

and fill my thoughts.

Though I'd like to know

where the path might finally go,

to find the one who hidden talks,

midst leaf and tree...field and fox.

.GB.

Notes

Dance

Some years ago I was walking in Seattle and saw a gyrating activity. People were gathered around the man in the middle of the activity. I asked a person standing nearby what was going on to discover that the man was doing a dance named "Butoh".

The underpinnings of the dance are not obvious, but the outward manifestations of Butoh are fascinating. Pain is the aim of the dance. The greater the pain the greater the dance. Amazing!

.GB.

Dance

Pain,

Palliated in play.

Gnawing, restless

...relentless.

Twisting, within a savage peace.

Lying,

Leaping,

Beaten,

Butoh!

.GB.

Notes

The Unsailed Sea

Everyone has crossed points in life that determined where their life would go. Vocations pursued, jobs chosen, people who became friends, locations, issues of faith, marriage, health issues and much more.

Looking back one muses about what might have been. It might be somewhat useless to one's practical life, but looking back has the possibility of charting a future.

Though a certain choice led into a resultant future, it can also inform a person about future choices that will be made.

The world appreciates Frost's poem that takes us to a fork of the road. Frost took the fork less travelled by and stated that it made all the difference. But who really knows the outcomes?

I appreciate the poem by Ella Wheeler Wilcox that notes one's course is determined by the set of the sail rather than the wind or the gale.

Still, one wonders, "What if a different direction had been chosen...what might have been?"

.GB.

The Unsailed Sea

There was a life, long ago

that lay like an unsailed sea.

A long look back

begs a clue,

to an untold mystery.

'tis where the heart hoists its sail

that charts its wish to be,

and speaks the truth

of an unpenned tale

waiting yet...in memory.

.GB.

Notes

O-Honey-O

This poem was written to express the times and feelings of young guys tapped to enter service through the draft in the Vietnam era.

As a veteran I was exposed to the angst of life when called to leave someone at home, and to face a future of death, injury and trauma. It's a hard walk...it's good to be home.

.GB.

O-Honey-O

Bella Anna Honey O,

where did ya go?

Songs sung so long ago,

just for you O Honey O.

Winds blew, winds blew so,

Caesar called, I had to go.

Where life led I didn't know.

Just a boy, not long from play,

far from my Honey O.

War marched to and fro,

I had to go, I had to go O Honey O.

Would a day come to stay

where a path led back...or go away?

I could not truly know,

oh my Bella Anna Honey O.

.GB.

Notes

Old Friends

This old poet has come to an age when the people who gather as friends begin to complain of heart trouble, difficulty in taking a breath, cancer, neuropathy and joints that ache.

Friends make life better. The presence of friends is like oxygen.

I implore my friends to stay well, and I will do my best to return the friendship given to me.

.GB.

Old Friends

Friends draw dear as we age,
yet,
our lists grow low on every page.

Each one holds a part of me,
to make my life much fuller be.

The loss of a friend, even one,
is the loss of myself in total sum.

So, take care of yourself my dear friend,
and like your garden do health attend.

For the life you share is a sacred seed,
planted in me by word and by deed.

I shall hoe my row, to be there for you,
and turn the soil in a word, or two.

If I can but one flower be,
I'll bloom bright and share with thee.

.GB.

Notes

La Mia Giulietta

All love stories seem to intersect with the timeless story of Romeo and Juliet. It is a story known to everyone, even to those who know nothing of Shakespeare's other works.

This poem purloins the bard's timeless play to express the love between two lovers who have been together a lifetime.

There is a sense of love that becomes even more dear as the years pass.

We might ask, how can love become stronger as we lose the fire and energy of youth? The answer is...it does!

Romeo and Juliet is only the beginning. The unwritten story of life is filled with such love, a love that is good, strong and true.

.GB.

La Mia Giulietta

I remember yesterday,
years where we formed and grew,
framed with golden light,
the light I see in you.
Holding on so dearly,
to love that brought us through,
you the Capulet and I a Montague.
Reflections in old memories,
those we longer hold, I see now clearly,
as later years unfold.
Lean on me in all the new tomorrows,
calming fears, and flooding sorrows.
Here I offer with gleaming band
the wholeness of my heart
and my loving hand.
Rise with me to spend this day,
on the path we early knew.
For this path leads one way
...to this golden love,
so good, so strong, so true.

.GB.

Notes

A New Day

There are moments, perhaps days and weeks that we are simply at our wits end. Our world has consumed us, and we are not able to cope. We plead, and we figuratively bleed. We laugh at our plight and we cry.

We come to points that have no acceptable solution.

Robert Frost advised us in his commentary to say that, *time marches on, tomorrow...the future comes, even when we are not ready.*

Today is not the end. In the midst of despair we can make plans to implement our hopes.

There is a tomorrow for which we have the opportunity to plan.

An old saying states that failure is never final.

.GB.

A New Day

Sometimes we beg, sometimes we plead,

sometimes, we simply bleed.

Sometimes we laugh, sometimes we cry.

It's usually best to dry our eye.

Pick up the pieces and get on our way,

'cause sunshine tomorrow spells a new day.

.GB.

Notes

Masks

It's the little things that cut, hurt, twist, rob, and kill the spirit that courtrooms never see. But they include crimes against truth, decency, help and honor. Little crimes can cut deep and injure. We are aware of such crimes. The only defense as stated by Saint Paul is to live with love, joy, peace, patience, kindness, generosity, faithfulness and self-control.

M. Scott Peck wrote a whole book titled *People of the Lie.* In it he points out that at its core, a mask, a façade is a lie. In it he states, *Truth is not something we possess; it is a goal toward which we hopefully strive.*

In his book Peck quotes Dr. Charles K. Robinson of Duke University who wrote, *God created you, God has seen our ugliness. God knows our sufferings and sees our beauty.*

Writer Keith Miller in his book *A Taste of New Wine,* states, *I believe that we deceive ourselves about our selfishness and egocentricity because we are afraid a revelation of our true nature would alienate us from our chosen associates.*

Peck acknowledges that love is the antidote to removing the mask and allows a new light to shine in us...

.GB.

Masks

Crime committed every day,

not in any headline way,

escapes the public law

but, yields an aching deeper flaw.

Thorns of imperfection

avoid discovery or detection.

Guile, deceit, duplicity

cover motive and malignancy.

Stolen treasure includes time,

yet, all crime leaves a sign

in the shadow of the shady goal

where a mask hides the soul.

.GB.

Notes

Arrow

Arrows are symbols of direction and velocity in life. Somewhere along our life's journey we begin to choose, and discover that life moves quickly. Target selection is crucial.

Discovering a purpose in life is one of life's major blessings.

The poem visualizes the arrow as life, velocity comes from the bow, the connection to the arrow is the string. All three come together to form the dynamic of life. Tension makes the string useful. As the arrow flies the string quivers.

...We are the archer; we pick the target.

Hitting the target is gratifying. Missing the target is disappointing. But, we have the opportunity to pick new directions, new purpose and new pursuits in life.

How fast flies the arrow of life...!

.GB.

Arrow

I placed the shaft

upon the bow

and arched it where

life might go.

To there soon this

quickened thing

flew

'tween measured mark

and quivering string.

.GB.

Notes

As Petals Fall

As we go through life we see changes. Time forces change. We look into mirrors and see a changed person from time to time.
There are times when we wonder about the future, and times when we look back with thanks and nostalgia.
This poem acknowledges that life is passing and expresses a hope that someone still holds us in their heart. As we remember special people, a special person or a special time, they are blessed, and so are we.

.GB.

As Petals Fall

As petals fall from the rose,

who knows where life goes?

Sage and saint, star and strong

ponder how we came along.

Yet, each petal one by one,

drops away as life is done,

that time to time, from hidden nook,

finds pressed petal in a book,

remembered for the life it had,

and all the times that made us glad.

With hope we wish our petal missed,

and, in someone's heart again be kissed.

As petals fall from the rose,

begs yet still where life goes.

.GB.

Notes

Bumping Seventy

I always wondered what it would be like to be seventy years old.
It always sounded like people dropped off the face of the earth at
seventy.

Much to my surprise I discovered seventy to be a wonderful age.
Most of our agility, physical and mental are still working...just a bit
slower.

Seventy is a different place, a time to reflect a bit, a time to
pursue things set aside in the bustle of life, a time to ease back a
bit and have that second cup of coffee...every day.

Seventy is an age where one can look back...and still look ahead.

.GB.

Bumping Seventy

Bumping seventy and still alive,
won't be old 'til seventy-five.
It's good to be young, these many years
midst life's struggles and withering fears.

If, when eighty, I'm still alive,
a new car I'll buy and take a drive.
The road now is not too long,
and whatever the route I can't go wrong.

For I've already been to places of worth
spanning the world on old mother earth.
And, with you, my love at my side,
I'm up for the day. Let's go for a ride.

.GB.

Notes

The Pilgrim Soul

Pilgrims take on a life as a mission of discovery...despite the risks. William Butler Yeats offers a line in one of his poems that reads, *When you are old and gray and full of sleep...one man loved the pilgrim soul in you.*

What did he mean? What is the pilgrim soul?

This poet thinks the pilgrim soul is a soul that looks for honesty, for truth and for authenticity despite the cost.

The reward comes in discovery, truth and finding other pilgrims along the way.

The pilgrim often finds that the pilgrim journey is a lonely uphill journey, but the view from the summit is awesome.

.GB.

The Pilgrim Soul

Looking down the length life,

with all its raw and scoured strife

finds the pilgrim soul.

Searching for a heart of honesty

staring down one's mendacity

purges pure the pilgrim soul.

As the bells of Mary toll,

and Buddha begs to fill his bowl

comes moksha to the soul.

All the paths of wandering,

all the thoughts and wondering

every peak its summiting

...lifts the pilgrim soul.

.GB.

Notes

The Poet Senses

Where, one might ask, does a poet find things to write about? There are partial answers. The poet has a sleepless eye that observes the world, and is always taking notes. Everything is within the reach of poetic interpretation.

Poetry is a way of presenting a thought, a way of interpreting history, a way of speaking from the deepest part of the human mind. Poetry can be precise, and it can relate to anything, it has no boundary.

Something stirs, words are formed, lines are written. The source is as mysterious as Beethoven writing a concerto and conducting it while deaf.

Language...expression, is a technical outcome of the wish to communicate. How it develops is like the formation of diamonds. Form and processes subject carbon to eons of pressure. It is a miracle. So, to, sounds become formed through time. Words are eventually formed, and thought is shared. Eventually words are strung together to speak not only of human need, but deeper thoughts fly in the mind to form expressions that go far beyond the rules of language.

The poet senses and reaches for words that express things that drive deep a point, things that tickle the gizzard, things that confess love, and an endless list of things rambling around in the mind of the poet.

.GB.

The Poet Senses

The poet senses, informed by a watching eye

that is always awake,

...disturbed by something almost visceral.

Emptiness is suddenly filled

by a compulsion to forge words,

words that reflect rage and peace,

warmth and passion,

fortune and failure,

love and loss.

Words to scream and cry,

words to whisper love

words that dance and play

words an inner awe doth belie.

.GB.

Notes

Coronation

Neume, from Medieval Latin, a group of notes sung in one breath. Neumes are simple fast notes designed in the neumorphic style. The point is speed not content. It is a short musical run. The term neume is ancient, usually associated with Gregorian chants.

Whispered words have great uplifting...healing power. Coronations of life can be passed to people that the world will never see, but they have the ability to lift up, making all the difference. They are coronations at the personal level. We are given as many crowns as we wish to give.

.GB.

Coronation

Vacant neumes will never still

songs of work or our freewill.

Prayers of blessing bring hope and health

...confer goodness, our real wealth.

Words whispered have the power to be

coronations of life crowned secretly.

.GB.

Notes

Bubbles

A bit obscure, our hopes are fragile, like a bubble of soap.

We have our hopes. Maybe hope is as far as our thoughts go, but hope is energy to approach an issue, to encircle it and nurture it until it becomes a reality.

.GB.

Bubbles

Penned lines...
    Like bubbles of soap
Drawn from breath
    to literally float
...on arcs of air
    from some subtle stroke
tracing transparent
    to lightly invoke
circling thoughts
    reflecting my hope.

.GB.

Notes

Cards and Candles

The heartfelt line of this poem is "Happy Birthday". Every time we hear these words another candle has been added to the cake.

As the poem states, every year is a win that gives us the privilege of life, its obligation, its opportunity, and its joys.

.GB.

Cards and Candles

A heartfelt line, meant to last,

lighting one wick more.

Chancing ways to live our days,

but, seldom keeping score.

Each year a win, a gift,

another treasured mile.

With much to do, friends to meet,

and mirth to make us smile.

.GB.

Notes

Audation

Audation is not meant to be an animistic poem, but rather was written in response to a realization that the miracle of nature has its own revelation of life.

It is often in the wood where the sounds of the world are muted and words, thoughts and feelings emerge.

Perhaps that is why we go on retreats where we enter a time of silence...something emerges, something happens when we become still and recognize that we hear something that speaks in the innermost part of ourselves.

.GB.

Audation

A breath, or was it there
a leaf went whispering?
As I thought I heard
a quiet passing word.
Yet, there was no one near,
no one that I could hear.
Still, I knew I'd heard
something like a spoken word.
Could it really be
that I'd heard a hidden tree?
Somewhere in the leafy wood
on a path I understood,
something of the subtle way,
the spirit, my spirit yields to pray.
Through thoughts drawn to deepening,
bosks lost in murmuring,
something said in furthering
...creation's mystery.

.GB.

Notes

A Word, Maybe Two

Sometimes we are overcome by too many words, too much opinion, too much advise.

A listening ear, gestures of concern and support suffice.

This poem was written in acknowledgement of active listening where being on target is better than a barrage of words.

.GB.

A Word, Maybe Two

An apt word will really do,

just one word, maybe two.

To help a bit don't take the stage,

or start a word and give a page.

Listen, give an ear,

perhaps a smile, or a tear.

Words can be so very few,

to be of help and stay on cue.

.GB.

SEASONS

Notes

Enuma Elis

Enuma Elis is an ancient Babylonian creation myth. It originated near the place often referred to as the cradle of civilization. We do not know how life began, or exactly where it began. We acknowledge that we are here, and even that is subject to much conjecture.

Creation stories are found in every civilization, and one thing is common to all creation stories. We were created, and we are not the preeminent power in the universe. There is a greater "other" that controls the essence of our being.

Most religions have a spiritual map that goes beyond our earthly journey. We take it in faith that there is more than this earthly life. In that faith I think of all the people I would like to see again. There are a lot of people on my list.

It will take a long time to see everybody. Since time is not of an essence in the new creation there lives a hope to deepen many-many old relationships.

In this wish there is a hope that there will be a time when the urgency and obligations of life are set aside, a day somewhere in the veiled future that will provide an opportunity to share a moment of quiet and peace with those who are a refuge.

While in this present time I ponder what waits. Wondering, I hope to amble along and speak of things that come from the heart and live in the soul.

I believe in a new reality, a new creation expressed here in poetry.

.GB.

Enuma Elis

When I enter the maw of time,

after fear and fire are done,

where souls need no breath,

nor earth, or sky, or sun.

May God grant a single day

to amble at your side.

Where rivers meet to run as one,

coursing deep, giving good,

whispers... ne'er expressed

but, understood,

forever saved to say.

Where moons no longer shine

or heaven's circles sway,

somewhere, beyond the pale of time,

waits...

...a new creation day.

.GB.

Notes

Wending Leaves

There is a lesson in the falling of leaves, for they are analogous to life. Each fall leaves float to the ground in profusion. One might think a leaf simply falls beneath the tree that bore the leaf, and so it is until the wind whisks the leaf from its landing place to some new place, and then the wind is not done with the leaf carries it further and further again and again...life carries us.

Perhaps as this poem was written it became an ode to life, an acknowledgement of the unpredictability of life, its trial and trouble. And, yet, out of such an odyssey life can be enriched, stretched, fulfilled.

The very things that challenge us are the things from which our character grows. It is the thing that allows us to rise above the quotidian.

.GB.

Wending Leaves

Leaves fell so softly down
somewhere upon a waiting ground.
As hands they held a tiny place
'til wind welled, to leave no trace.

I thought again another day
of leaves that now so gently lay
and wonder where the wind might will
to carry them yet further still.

Life or leaf the wind will blow
to set some course that we will go.

What we do when we are free
as leaves befallen from the tree,
comes not from our own hand,
or from all we understand.

There wells a wind to come some day
to change our choice or what we may.
For life denies one's full command
to even kings who can demand.

The wind, the wind that lifts the breeze
brings change to life as to the leaves.

When, rend we then to some new place
where wind or wile will leave no trace
of what laid last, now behind
waits yet, to the future find.

.GB.

Notes

Tulips In April

Tulips In April has long been a favorite of mine. It is written to celebrate spring and the joy of the season. I dedicate this poem to April babies, especially to a baby born on the first burst of April personifying the very essence of spring. April is an exciting month. More poetry is written celebrating the advent of spring and April than any other month.

If you are an April baby, this poem is for you...and for spring!

.GB.

Tulips In April

You are tulips in April
and roses in May.
sunflowers in August,
and daisies today.

I would hold you in bunches
and, dance in your arms,
to breathe your fine fragrance
and kiss your sweet charms.

You name every flower,
and by name each do know,
'mid stobs and stakes,
row upon row.

You are there...
I see your face,
and find in each flower
the essence of grace.

So mine is the gift
you've given to me
to see in each field.
acres of thee.

.GB.

Notes

The Spring of '06

It was a good spring. The snow was finally gone. Buttercups were up and the whole armamentarium of nature was poised to burst into bloom.

We wait...we wait, and then on a warm day the world explodes into color with all its breathtaking array.

It is spring, and in '06.   I picked up my pen and jotted a note on what I saw...and, deeply felt.

.GB.

The Spring of '06

Spring!

The wet and waiting sod
      tempts root, bud and bursting pod.

The spring is come all around,
      stretched out green on fecund ground.

There, on a flowered clod
      bluebell, rose and goldenrod.

It arrived one warming day,
      panting life, bees at play.

God breathed,
      Earth turned,
         Again, spring...on display!

.GB.

Notes

April First

April First is a poem of celebration. The days around April first are days of high anticipation. The world, my world, is bursting with life. William Shakespeare wrote Sonnet XVIII in which he described summer as a time following "The darling buds of May". April is the true beginning of spring. It announces the healing hand of nature. How glad I am when winter's frost has finally passed and the celebration of spring begins.

Gaea is mythological, a primordial goddess of the earth.

.GB.

April First

I celebrate April first,
casting calm on winter's worst,
cold days disappear,
to sing of spring
whose warm winds bring
summer's sabbath near.

Crocus, bell and buttercup,
always first appear,
then daffodil and tulips up
...spear by spear by spear.

Gardens green into bloom,
sunshine sweetens rain,
Gaea gasps aloud again,
with nature in refrain.

April always gladdens me,
bud and blossomed tree,
when, buzz begins
in every pollened bee,
and life breathes, deep and free.
...year by year by year.

.GB.

Notes

Winter Wills

Winter has always brought cold and ice. And, as people grow older the winter world gets harder to negotiate. Getting groceries becomes a challenge. Shoveling snow, driving on icy roads, walking on icy pathways make winter more hazardous.

There was a time when winter meant skiing, sledding, snow men, ice skating and a time of gift giving. Winter was a season of fun. It was also a season of wet clothes and chilblain.

Spring is received with welcome. In spring life abounds!
But, in recent years summer has become a time of fire, smoke filled air and choking haze. Some states are burning down.

Now, winter has become a refuge from the vagaries of summer. The earth becomes pristine. The air is pure, the earth regains its ancient charm. Snow fills the mountains so that summer water continues to flow.

There is a new found peace about winter.

.GB.

Winter Wills

Winter wills,
To wash the droughted land
And cool the burning sand.
Winter wills to bring its shorter days
And clear the smokey haze.
Winter welds the world with ice
Where fire cannot entice
Sparks that burn earth's trees
on Ana's blazing breeze.
Hushed days, cold nights,
Bears sleep, snows greet.
Winter wills.

.GB.

Notes

Pasque

Passover is an important celebration in the life of congregations around the world. It celebrates the exodus of the Hebrews from slavery. The exodus took place in the month of Nisan which comes in the spring of the year.

As the exodus represents deliverance from slavery, spring is a deliverance from winter. It is a time of hope, fulfilled dreams, warmth and freedom. The Seder and spring are celebrated because both are celebrations of life.

Much of the ancient Hebrew tradition is preserved in songs that are derived from the origins of poetry. The Psalms of the Old Testament, the songs of Miriam, the songs of Deborah, the song of Lamech, David's laments, The song of the well. Songs drawn from experiences of historical proportions as well as from daily life, The song of Solomon, Genesis 4.23-24, Exodus 15.21, Numbers 21.17, Judges 5, Second Samuel 1.19-27, Amos 6.5, Psalms 137.3-4.

The Psalms reflect in a timeless way the universal aspirations, doubts, fears and issues of the human heart. Hebrew poetry did not concern itself so much with meter or rhyme, the chief style of their poetry was rhythm and couplets or verse of two lines of about equal length, the second line completing or contrasting the first line which appears in *Pasque*. See Job 28.12-28, Proverbs 8.12-26 and Psalm 104.

Today, in Temple a cantor sings the songs and the congregation sings the Amens. At the heart of all of the Psalms and folk music of the Church is a great thanksgiving for deliverance from slavery...

.GB.

Pasque

To see the bud

betree again.

Bare limb and stem

to green again.

The air to

dare repair again.

My dreams to rise

alive again.

...deliverance

.GB.

THE EBB

Notes

Deep Water

Life is not a trip across a serene sea where one sits on a deck chair enjoying warm sun and a gentle breeze. Life is filled with challenge...from birth. We are in charge of our lives. Circumstances, personal deficits, limitations, locations, events, peer groups and institutions determine our life. We struggle, negotiate, compromise, stumble, push on, look for help, and often go it alone.

Chaos, unpayable debt, fear, lack of core beliefs, lack of accountability and criminality and lives out of control are icons of a dystopian culture. We are free to do anything, but not really free because choices have consequences, conveniences and modern advancements, life continues to be a place of danger and potential destruction...deep water.

This poem does not belong in this book of poems reflecting warmth, love, security and inclusion. But it was chosen to acknowledge the part of the world that can destroy and devour human souls.

.GB.

Deep Water

To all the ships that sovereign sail,
'tween biting wind and bitter gale,
with chartless maps that cannot see
rock rimmed cliffs of destiny.
How vast the sea,
how vast the sea that starless be.
Wild the winds untutored path
churning deep life's daunting grasp.
But, sail they must those raw and nee,
launched untied, but, never free.
No true captain, crew or mate
to turn the boats from certain fate.
And so, we wait, we wait to see
if by chance safe passage be.
Yet, rock and rain also wait
...on life's surging sea.

.GB.

Notes

Valedictory

Valedictory was written to a friend, my oldest friend, with whom I had not corresponded for some time.

As time passed I felt an urgency to write and share something of the times we shared, times that hold warm memories and are deeply valued.

Valediction is the act of bidding farewell. It is a time of saying last things, and I hoped for the opportunity to reminisce, to savor those years long ago. I have written three or four poems expressing this sentiment. The friend for whom these poems were written passed away this year, and the time to share the past did not happen.

There is for all of us an urgency to reach out to share a valedictory moment.

My friend is not of this world now, but he lives on, and those memories still warm my heart.

.GB.

Valedictory

Life lives breath to breath,
then, sighs a subtle change.
From scene-to-scene seasons green
where memories fully range.

In seeds that creep
from somewhere deep
rising now to grow,
midst the weeds of undone deeds,
comes new greens in row.

Why some ask beget this task
since years and years
have quietly passed?

Because it's time, the moments here,
to share these things,
the way is clear.

So now, old friend
let's speak of things
borne on wings and blessed.

This season cast
perhaps the last,
words to be confessed.

.GB.

Notes

Valentine

Valentine's Day is a special day. It has become a day to express love, a day when we say thank you to friends, a day when love is expressed in candy, flowers and cards.

Somewhere around the second century Christians named Valentines (named after the martyrdom of the one now named Saint Valentine) were martyred and the day has been remembered.

There are other stories as well. Now, Saint Valentine's Day is celebrated on February 14th each year.

This poem was written to acknowledge the omission of the husband's appreciation or love on Valentine's Day for someone I know well. And, to recognize and encourage the love she gives to others in so many small ways throughout the year.

.GB.

Valentine

There came today nothing sweet
No word, no touch, no mot nor treat.

No flower stem from Cupid's bow,
It was a day you've come to know.

But, time was given fair to thee,
For in it you are fully free

To bend the bow upon its string,
And give to life the love you bring.

The memories that now you save,
Arrived today...in what you gave.

.GB.

Notes

At the End

The ache at the loss of a dear friend is hard. We are disarmed, there are no words to heal. There is only emptiness.

I have experienced it, as have so many-many.

.GB.

At The End

Today, morphine laced with propofol

to 'suage the ache the final wall.

Remembering your laugh,

a laugh that lingers, from our last call.

Tears flood my eyes, time has ceased to be.

Fear claims you... and sorrow has me.

.GB.

Notes

The Day Will Come

There is always a future day in our lives that we leave behind people who have meant so very much to us. Memories are what we leave, and for those we have loved it is hoped that we will be remembered well.

Poetry is replete with verse that speaks of this. In her poem *To a Friend,* Amy Lowel writes, *"I ask but one thing of you...that I will be my dream of you."*

If I think of things true...it will be the thought of you...gb

.GB.

The Day Will Come

The day will come
...as you must know
that you will stay and I will go.
To changing skies and chartless fields
where nothing's sure
...the spirit wields.
Sharing things never dared,
thinking things never shared,
...waiting.
Glancing up where thoughts arise
chancing life's daunting tries,
...hoping
that you might pass this way
on a welcome future day,
that as I go you will know
...you will know.

.GB.

Notes

Click

The click here is the sound of a door closing. Doors close in life. Circumstances close doors.   Misunderstandings close doors.

Sometimes, a door closes as a result of hurt feelings, deceit or embarrassment.

A closed door often leaves no opportunity to remove the barrier of a door closed to us.

The poem faces such a door, and expresses the pain of it.

.GB.

Click

I heard a click,

then saw a door

quietly close to me.

To open nevermore,

nevermore will be

a word shared

evermore with thee.

.GB.

Notes

Gone

The notes that accompany this poem come more as prayer than as commentary. It is written out of the times I have been with friends and family after a separation, death or dissolution of a marriage or relationship. It is written with a particular person in mind, someone quite dear to me. It has been a hard time for her.

The prayer is written with a man in mind, and the deep angst he is feeling:

God...I've just had a fight with my wife. I can't remember how it started, but there is now a gulf between us. Speak to me the words that will help to cross the void, and help me to speak them with the love I feel for her.

Whatever the issue there is between us, it is nothing compared to the love I feel for her. Help me to listen to her words without judgement, and let me speak with words of support and understanding   Amen.

.GB.

Gone

Once she had a home,
  but, backed a bit away.
Bit by bit some time ago,
  day, by day, by day.
Though in a house,
  that's not her truest home.
Home is not a house,
  but a love to call one's own.
Today the doors are closed,
  cold like winter's stone.
There is no sunny side,
  just empty rooms...alone.
Waiting for the day,
  a door be found ajar,
  with sun to warm her heart,
  in hope, this day will not be far.

.GB.

Notes

Miss Ya Bill

Miss Ya Bill is a poem that looks back at my life in a small township named Curlew. They were happy days. I lived in the midst of cousins who were my closest friends.

We did the things in this poem every day. We spanned ages seven and five, some a bit older, some a bit younger, but we had each other.

It was a privilege to be a part of it.

.GB.

Miss Ya Bill

On the river floatin' boats
Slappin' cow pies, throwin' ropes
Fixin' Kool Aid 'n layin' back 'gainst a wall
Chippin' ice 'neath a sawdust quay
Coolin' tongues on summer's day
Curlew creeks and beaver ponds
Fished with worms and willow wands
Walkin' down the railroad track
All the way down and all the way back
What did we talk about all that time?
You 'bout seven, me bout' five.

.GB.

Notes

The Second Step

I do not easily handle goodbyes. It seems that visits end too soon, though a few days is time enough to catch up on all the news, and time enough to get a sense of a friend's inner world.

The poem is a pattern, my inner pattern, at parting.

Within minutes of parting I am left with the memory of the visit.

Good visits usually leave a resolve to continue the visit again...in the future.

The poem was written in response to a particular sadness in parting.

.GB.

The Second Step

I went on a bit and turned

to see you wave,

Then, another step

that soon became a mile.

I turned again,

now, only the path

and, the vision of your smile.

.GB.

Notes

At the End

Ache of a lost friendship, a lost relationship is hard. We are disarmed, there are no words to heal. There is only emptiness.

It hurts, it aches. It comes to us all and saddened one continues on.

.GB.

At The End

Quiet now,

only a colic void,

no heated word.

A day strayed,

and then another,

and when I turned to speak

you were not there.

Only the echoes

of a lost friendship

remain.

.GB.

CHEEKS

Notes

Liz II

Elizabeth II was queen for 96 years, from 6 February 1952 until 8 September 2022. She lived for 96 years and reigned in dignity, strength and grace. She was loved by her people and held in the highest respect by the world.

.GB.

Liz II

Queen you were,
Right from the start.
And, friend
You became,
Deep in my heart.

.GB.

Notes

Dithering

How often have we gone around wringing our hands over some unaccountable thing only to realize not only the futility of worry, but the thing itself is fast fading from our memory?

.GB.

Dithering

Went to the window

went to the door,

wandered around

pacing the floor.

Couldn't remember,

began to doubt,

worrying more

feelings in rout.

Gotta be tough,

gotta be stout,

gotta recall

what it's about.

.GB.

Notes

Doodle Dust

For some unexplained reason I am compelled to write something in the dust on a chest of drawers, or on a table top. Sometimes steam on a mirror invites me to write a brief thought on it.

It must be some primal thing, there is no other explanation.

.GB.

Doodle Dust

In doodle dust my fingers twine

there to scribe some silly rhyme.

Waiting for the polish cloth

to come along and wipe it off.

But still, there is this wanting urge

I cannot fight or even purge.

Compelled to jot a trifling thought

on pads of dust...that doodling wrought.

.GB.

Notes

True Royalty

What man has not come to a moment such as this. He is in the presence of a most desirable woman, and realizes that she has looked at him. The look is the first step to an encounter. It is the genesis of an urging. But, in it there is the possibility of rejection or a look of dismissal. The male ego hopes to be gratified with the same outcome hoped for by the frog of the fable, the frog that wanted to become a prince through a kiss.

There is no short-cut. The moment always hangs in the balance. We wait for a nod, a long look, a proverbial drop of the hankie...something!

The kiss assures the heart...perhaps the ego, and we are, at least in the moment granted royalty.

.GB.

True Royalty

Her quiet eyes looked at me,
  What there did she see?

Prince, I yearned to be.
  Frog, I feared, most inwardly.

Waiting with a daunting wish,
  to leap across the dark abyss.

Lifted by a loving kiss,
  Tapped for true royalty.

.GB.

Notes

Dating

Working up the courage to ask someone for a date is no small thing, and it is possible to think about a date only to put it off.

This short poem gets to the point.

.GB.

Dating

Alaska, Nebraska,

t' date

cha gotta aska.

.GB.

Notes

Non-Sequitur

The mother in this poem is my own. She had a wit that showed up...often.

The reference to the little girl with a little curl, always amused my mother. She would quote it, and my brother and I would shout out, "When she was good, she was very-very good, but when she was bad, she was horrid." Then we would all laugh.

In life she was a serious person. As a young person she was a violinist in the Tacoma Symphonic Orchestra, Eagle Scout, and climbed Mount Rainier at age 16. As an adult she was a high school English teacher, and Commercial Arts teacher. She taught high school until her retirement.

Mom had a funny bone. She loved Betty White and Phyllis Diller. Mom would have made a great stand-up comic. She never aspired to be one, but she turned out to be a stand-up comic at home and around friends.

.GB.

Non-Sequitur

Momma used to say
When impish and at play
"There was a girl
With a little curl,
Right in the middle of her forehead".
She loved the absurd,
Or, convoluted word,
Especially in a rhyme
To share anytime.
Before she was done
We'd blurt out in fun
"And, when she was bad she was horrid!"
Momma had a funny bone
Even when alone,
But, she always liked to share
Sayings very rare
To simply get a rise
Much to our surprise.
She loved Betty White
And, in Diller did delight.
She could have been another.
But, life being life,
Became a stand-up mother.

.GB.

Notes

Miracles

Miracles makes an audacious statement. To say that miracles are the only sure things in life is a tall order, even if stated in poetry. Certainly not everything is a miracle, nor is doubt that asserts that nothing is a miracle.

Existence, nobody can explain where everything came from.

Kindness that comes from people who have suffered great abuse.

Generosity that comes from those with nothing.

Light that banishes darkness.

Healing that provides wellness.

Breath that gives life.

The swell of life that inhabits Earth.

Minds that ponder the universe.

Some might offer that all that we call a miracle is just ordinary.

Nay...it's a miracle.

.GB.

Miracles

Within

the

midst

of

stress

and

strife,

miracles

are

the

only

sure

things

in life.

.GB.

Notes

Scribbled Knots

Scribbled Knots is a poem only one sentence long. And, yet, it is descriptive of that inner place where poetry resides, and the place from which poetry comes.

In her book *Thorn Birds,* Colleen McCullough poignantly states, *Each of us has something within us that won't be denied, even if it makes us scream to die.*

In her book the mythical thorn bird seeks for the perfect tree of thorns where it lies upon a thorn and sings its last and most beautiful song while in the throes of death. Such is the writing of poetry.

.GB.

Scribbled Knots

...and, so, I write in scribbled knots

Of deep felt words and hidden thoughts.

.GB.

Notes

Barrels

Barrels was written for the cooks and lovers of condiments. The poem is pure whimsy.

Salt was mined six thousand years ago in the area in and around Romania. It was also mined in China. Salt is mentioned in the history of the ancient Hebrews, Hittites, Egyptians, Byzantines, Romans and in India. It is essential to human health and tantalizes the tastebuds.

To have a barrel of salt in ancient days was to be rich. Even recent history notes that a struggle between the people of India and Great Britain was over the issue of salt.

The poem is whimsy, but salt is serious.

As for pepper, it is the worlds most traded spice. A little-known fact reveals that pepper is made from the drupe of the pepper plant before it is ripe, "serious business".

.GB.

Barrels

Barrels of salt,

cases of Pepper,

now I can season

forever and ever.

.GB.

Notes

Time

Time is a mystery. It cannot be seen or heard. It is the measure of everything. It is not the same in one place as it is in another. Velocity changes time, but time continues, endlessly, and we cannot escape it. Time is a mystery.

The author of Ecclesiastes in the Old Testament spoke of time as a season: A time for every matter under heaven. *A time to be born and a time to die; a time to plant and a time to reap, a time to take life and a time to heal; a time to break and a time to build; a time to laugh and a time to cry; a time to mourn and a time to dance; a time to set up camp and a time to move on; a time for love and a time for business; a time to speak and a time for silence.*

Only the present moment is available to us, a silent gift in which we are given the opportunity to select the subject and set the predicate.

.GB.

Time

Sand fell

without a chime,

a soundless tick

echoed time.

.GB.

Notes

Toodle Loo

At the end of each week, just before quitting time I enjoyed sending the staff a short poem. *Toodle Loo* struck me as a way to say goodbye in one of my weekly offerings.

It suggests a "goodbye" that is not going to be long...just a stepping out until we see each other again.

The poem spans the weekend, we will be together again on Monday where they will again be inflicted with my whimsy.

Until then, I simply say...toodle loo!

.GB.

Toodle Loo

This week is nearly through
...toodle loo.
And, so now this thing I do,
this posey ode I send to you.
I'm not sure I can explain
just why you endure this pain,
but for me it's very plain,
the fun I have is pure gain.
So, again I say to you,
toodle loo,
toodle loo,
toodle loo.

.GB.

Notes

The Sun Winked

The setting of this poem places it in the mountains where small lakes dot the landscape. The area is crisscrossed with paths, dirt roads and trails. The chance of meeting someone so early in the morning is remote, most folks are still in their sleeping bags or lighting a fire for breakfast.

By chance two people meet on their respective walks...the fisherman to a small pond and, the early morning walker to a path leading up a hill.

Will they meet again?

.GB.

The Sun Winked

Dawn's light lit the wood,

there did he a stranger meet.

Without a word through the mist

they did wordless greet.

Passed he then to the marsh

and she to the hill,

where rose the sun that seemed to say,

Would you come again this way?

To which he replied...*I will!*

.GB.

Notes

Rain

Haiku seemed to be the right form in which to write this poem. Rain falls vertically, thus the structure of this poem. Perhaps the poem could just as easily have been called *Falling.*

The subject of the poem is rain, but it is mostly about us. We come to moments in our lives when we simply fall, and there is nothing to catch us. And, as a drop of rain eventually lands somewhere, so do we.

It is when we land that we begin again...not like before, but to some new purpose in life. Like a drop of rain we are destined to find a new path, and eventually rise again.

.GB.

Rain

.

.

.

.

falls

and

falls

and

falls

and

falls

and

falls

and

falls

and

falls

and

falls

and

stops somewhere.

.GB.

Notes

Sticks and Stones

As children we encounter our peers who hurl words at us with the intention of hurting us. And, they do!

We report our injury to our mothers, who teach us the old aphorism...*but, words can never hurt us.* Ha! Fat chance of that!

Then we grow to become grown-ups, adults, level headed people, and recognize that the poem is just a nostrum. The truth is, words are the worst kind of weapon.

We grow thick skins, but hopefully we have soft hearts and hold back words that injure.

Not long ago a radio/TV personality let loose on a well-known women's soccer team. The world descended on him in hob-nail boots. He lost his job.

Sometimes we pay a price for hurling cuts at others, and sometimes the target of our words never forget the hurt.

As Dad used to say...*zip it.*

.GB.

Sticks and Stones

Sticks and stones

break our bones,

but, words can truly haunt us.

To curl the lip,

and let words slip

come back soon to bite us.

Words are flip, when they clip,

and cut cruel to slight us.

.GB.

Notes

O, the Rose

Short poems, a single line, sometimes gets right to the point. The fragrance of fresh cut roses brings a girl to mind who has brought me purpose, luck and happiness.

.GB.

O, the Rose

Poets say things in essence true, just as roses tell of you.

.GB.

Notes

Hello Fort Worth

My friend sold her house, the news came as a real surprise. She had owned the house for over thirty years. Her move elicited this short poem.

I'm glad she moved. It was time. And, the folks who will welcome her to Fort Worth are pure gold.

.GB.

Hello Fort Worth

My friend sold her house,

leaving quiet as a mouse.

In Joy, maybe mirth,

she heads to old Fort Worth.

Sold fast...Wow!

Just the closing,

and one final bow.

.GB.

Notes

Over Easy

I like my eggs cooked sunny-side up and then turned over easy. I
met a girl who cooks 'em this way. She flipped me. That's how
this poem came to mind.

The poem is a bit obscure. It is light-hearted. It's a poem that
playfully reaches out to her.

I hope she reads this poem and understands it...which is to go on
cookin' and flippin',

...my eggs so to speak.

.GB.

Over Easy

If

I

were

an

egg

I'd

like

to

be

sunny-side up

and

flipped

by

thee.

.GB.

Notes

Wednesday Next

There was a girl at a box social in a local church. She was beautiful, every eye was on her. She sat with the date that had brought her.

As the evening pressed on she looked at another fellow, the one writing this poem, with eyes that said, *hello*!

The incidents in this poem actually happened. The girl became the poet's wife. I'm the lucky guy...many years ago.

.GB.

Wednesday Next

It took a little while
to see that hidden smile.

Yet, I could not certify
if I did not try
to take a fleeting peek.

You laid your hand
across your cheek,
and revealed a dimple
as though to speak.

The dimple did me in.
So, I smiled back.

You quickly turned away,
just how quick I could not say,
but fast is fast and
a moment passed
before you looked back at me.

Well, that was that,
we began to chat,
and, soon agreed
to meet Wednesday next
              ...about three.

.GB.

Notes

Nee

Nee, is a bit of whimsy that makes a point. The Miller's son can provide the flour, but it is the Baker's daughter who brings forth new life...the greater thing!

.GB.

Nee

He was the Miller's son
and flour did he make,
but it took the Baker's daughter
to give the world a cake.

.GB.

Notes

Swishing

Swishing is a poet's nod to the great ranges of fish and swimming mammals like whales, porpoise and related animals. The poem is whimsy best suited for kids, kids of all ages.

It is reported by marine biologists that some fish swim from Alaska to Australia...some farther.

In my part of the world salmon swim deep into the ocean and return all the way back to the place in the creek where they were born.

The distance swished is measured in the thousands of miles...amazing!

.GB.

Swishing

There are fish, traveling fish,

That swim far in the salty sea,

as far as far can be.

To see the world shore to shore,

to isles great and wee,

For some fish there is a swish,

that swims fast, fast full and free.

If you are such a fish

that has this wish

great worlds you will see.

.GB.

Notes

Summer Magic

In the north summer is so grand that it seems to disappear in a blink. There are years when summer is reduced from its three month promise to just a few weeks in July and August.

The poem is my response to a spent summer.

Partly used bottles of suntan lotions, creams and sprays lie waiting in a bottom drawer, mute testimony to my yearning for a longer season.

.GB.

Summer Magic

Winter came
    and stayed a year,
Then summer
    came to play.
But, winter seems
    so ever near,
While summer
    lasts a day.

.GB.

Notes

Rose Red

From time to time it is fun to play with a tried and true rhyme. "Roses are red" is the beginning line for poems usually expressing love or something conveying humor. It is a way for someone to reveal a truth without committing to a deeper commitment. In the case of this poem the deeper connection is intended...while being casually offhanded.

Emily Dickinson made light of reference to roses as she wrote... *A flash of dew, a bee or two, petal, sepal, thorn...and I'm a rose. XCIII*

.GB.

Rose Red

Roses are red so true

so true

and, God kissed the world

when He made you!

.GB.

Notes

Nighttime Stories

Nighttime stories by Shadrach, Meshach and to bed you go is a play on words from the story of three men in the third chapter of the book of Daniel who safely walked through the flames of a fiery furnace. There was a fourth figure in the furnace thought to be the son of God.

.GB.

Nighttime Stories

by

Shadrach, Meshach

and

To Bed You Go.

.GB.

Notes

The Bite

Some bites are truly painful, lasting from days to a year, some last up to two years! Itching is the chief complaint. Experience has proven that the application of repellents and protective clothing do not stop these small creatures from finding my skin.

The worst are those that come at night while I lie defenseless in sleep,

Ouch!

.GB.

The Bite

Whether bitten

by bug or by bee,

makes no difference,

no difference to me.

Bites and stings

bring only pain,

a shout of alarm

is my only refrain.

Sadly, they come

and bite me to bits,

finding my fat,

giving me fits.

As I was having

a really fine day,

they found me at last,

and took it away.

.GB.

Notes

That's That

Society places a great deal of emphasis on being thin. Diets of all sorts suggest ways of attaining a trim figure, and medical science offers lists of ways to measure fat. There is the Body Measure Index, Bioelectric impedance Analysis, Hydrostatic Weighing and Dual Energy X-Ray Absorptiometry.

Dire warnings are all around us. But there comes a point where we simply don't care, and pick up an extra cookie, put cream in our coffee and eat the last scrap on an overflowing plate.

Shameless!

.GB.

That's That

Now we're old and big and fat

We say to all,
    ...well, that's that!

Oh, for bites butter rich,

And, sugared sweets that tear a stitch.

Some would have us thin one day,
    But we're content, just this way.

Now, we're old and big and fat
    To all we say,
        ...well, that's that!

.GB.

Notes

Abigail Gump

Young Abigail Gump is a wonderful character. She got a sting right on her pretty nose and with great embarrassment attempted to hide the evidence.

We all get some annoyance on our faces. Pimples, cold sores, bites, stings, scratches and so on.

Hiding them is the only thing we can do.

Abigail finally confessed. Poor little Abigail, I hope she recovers...soon!

.GB.

Abigail Gump

Young Abigail Gump had a lump
    she was loathe to disclose.
She got it one day
    while at play,
    crimson red, a rose.
Alarmed for her charm
    and what might be said
    (by her brother Fred)
    she hid it under her clothes.
Asked by those
    to fully disclose
    Abigail stared
    down, at her toes.
Under duress
    she finally confessed
    that she'd
      while tree'd
        been bee'd
right on her pretty nose.

.GB.

171

Notes

Pure Money

Have you ever noticed the women who host financial programs on television? Not only do they know a lot about stocks, bonds, options and equities, but they are attractive. They appear before the public looking like runway models.

It just proves that beauty and brains can come together... it's a great combination.

.GB.

Pure Money

I have a girl named Toots,

who trades calls and puts.

In a single trade,

ten thousand she made,

while doing her lipstick for looks.

.GB.

Notes

Minnie Muff

Cats, felis catus, domestic house kitties are sweet mousers that become little pals. They curl up next to us and beg to be rubbed under their chins and behind their ears.

It is estimated that there are over one hundred million kitties in the U.S.A. Historically house cats have been around for over ten millennia.

The term *pussy cat* can be traced back to the sixth century A.D. from the low German word *pusskatte*.

.GB.

Minnie Muff

I had a kiddy cat, her name was Minnie Muff
Outside she was a ball of fur, inside she was tuff.

.GB.